EARTH BY NUMBERS

Earth's Landforms

Nancy Dickmann

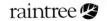
raintree
a Capstone company — publishers for children

Raintree is an imprint of Capstone Global Library Limited, a company incorporated in England and Wales having its registered office at 264 Banbury Road, Oxford, OX2 7DY – Registered company number: 6695582

www.raintree.co.uk
myorders@raintree.co.uk

Text © Capstone Global Library Limited 2019
The moral rights of the proprietor have been asserted.

Produced for Raintree by Calcium
Editors: Sarah Eason and Harriet McGregor
Designer: Paul Myerscough
Originated by Capstone Global Library Limited © 2018
Printed and bound in India

ISBN 978 1 4747 6535 0
22 21 20 19 18
10 9 8 7 6 5 4 3 2 1

British Library Cataloguing in Publication Data
A full catalogue record for this book is available from the British Library.

Acknowledgements
Picture credits: Cover: Shutterstock: BCampbell65; Insides: NASA: 11; Shutterstock: Marcos Amend 18, Thomas Barrat 14–15, Canadastock 6, ChrisVanLennepPhoto 17, Budkov Denis 9, Asaf Eliason 16, Marisa Estivill 20–21, Ammit Jack 8–9, Kavram 10, Andrzej Kubik 29, Doug Meek 26, R McIntyre 24–25, Alice Nerr 22–23, Mati Nitibhon 15, Pecold 22, Vadim Petrakov 18-19, Ralwel 4–5, Santi Rodriguez 26–27, Nicram Sabod 5, Susan Schmitz 1, 21, Konstantin Stepanenko 25, Szefei 28–29, Jolanta Wojcicka 12–13, YuG 6–7; Wikimedia Commons: 13.

Every effort has been made to contact copyright holders of material reproduced in this book. Any omissions will be rectified in subsequent printings if notice is given to the publisher.

Contents

Our amazing planet   4

Mountains and Valleys   6

Volcanoes   8

Mountains and volcanoes—
    by numbers!   10

Oceans   12

Lakes   14

Bodies of water—by numbers!   16

Rivers   18

Canyons   20

Rivers—by numbers!   22

Islands   24

Caves   26

A home for all   28

Glossary   30
Find out more   31
Index   32

Some words are shown in bold, **like this**. You can find out what they mean by looking in the glossary.

Our amazing planet

Our planet, Earth, is an amazing place. The land is covered with tall mountains and steep **cliffs**, winding rivers and calm lakes. It also has dry **deserts**, **fertile prairies** and lush **rainforests**. Even beneath the ground, cave systems stretch kilometres. The oceans are also full of life, and deep beneath the water's surface are features that look like those on the land: trenches, mountains and even **volcanoes**.

All of these amazing features are landforms, and they provide a wide range of **habitats** for Earth's many plants and animals. Landforms may seem permanent, but they are constantly changing, as new ones form and old ones disappear. When Earth was first formed, it looked very different. Millions of years of moving rock and water have shaped the planet we know today.

EARTH BY NUMBERS

Landforms are not only found on Earth. The Moon, for example, has mountains, valleys and plains. The rocky planets Venus and Mars are dotted with volcanoes.

Mars is home to a huge system of **canyons**, the Valles Marineris. It is almost as long as the United States is wide, and four times as deep as the Grand Canyon!

Beautiful oceans of liquid water cover more than two-thirds of Earth's surface.

Amazing **fjords**, such as this one in Norway, are formed by icy **glaciers** carving out the landscape.

Mountains and Valleys

Mountains are some of the most impressive landforms on Earth. Their towering peaks seem to stretch towards the sky. Many are so high that they are permanently covered with ice and snow. Earth's highest mountain, Mount Everest, is an amazing 8,848 metres (29,029 feet) tall. That's almost 11 times higher than the world's tallest building!

Earth's **crust** is made up of many smaller pieces called **tectonic plates**. These plates "float" on top of the softer **molten** rock inside Earth, like pieces of an eggshell. The plates are constantly moving, and when two plates push up against each other, mountains can form. The pressure of the two plates forces rock upwards in a process that can take millions of years. The uplifted rock forms a mountain range, with many individual peaks.

Many mountain valleys form an important habitat for plants and animals that are specially adapted to live there.

The Himalayas are the world's highest mountain range. They formed when the land that is now India collided with the rest of Asia. They are still growing.

EARTH BY NUMBERS

Between mountains or hills, you'll find valleys. These long, thin areas of lower ground can be formed in different ways. Some were carved out by the movement of huge glaciers.

Others were formed when a river made its way through, grinding down the rock and soil and then carrying it away. Many early humans settled in valleys.

Volcanoes

One type of mountain is a little more unpredictable than the others: volcanoes. These mountains can sometimes **erupt**, spewing out ash, gases and molten rock called **lava**. The lava eventually hardens to form new rock.

Some volcanoes form where two tectonic plates are moving away from each other, leaving a gap in Earth's crust. **Magma** rises from beneath to fill the gap. Other types of volcanoes are formed when two plates are pushed together. One plate is forced beneath another, forming a subduction zone. The sinking plate heats up and releases water, which helps to melt the rock. When this magma reaches the surface, volcanoes are formed.

A few volcanoes form over places called "hotspots". These are places where there is a large area of unusually hot rock beneath the surface. Hotspots beneath the oceans can form volcanic islands. The islands of Hawaii were formed in this way.

EARTH BY NUMBERS

When volcanoes erupt, they spew out molten rock called lava. Eruptions underneath water or ice make a type of lava called pillow lava. Above ground, lava that cools slowly, without moving too fast, will form pahoehoe. A type of lava called a'a cools more quickly while it is moving fast, forming a rough, jagged surface.

It is hard to tell when a volcano will erupt. Some can lie **dormant** for hundreds of years between eruptions.

The shape and texture of volcanic rock depends on how thick the lava was, and how quickly it cooled and hardened.

The Andes Mountains in South America stretch for more than 7,000 kilometres (4,350 miles) from north to south, with an average height of 3,960 metres (13,000 feet). Beneath the oceans, however, is a much longer chain: the mid-ocean ridge. It is more than

64,370

kilometres (40,000 miles) long.

On average, tectonic plates move at about

2.5 – 10

centimetres (1–4 inches) per year. That's about as fast as your fingernails grow!

Some mountains are growing taller in zones where tectonic plates are still pushing together. For example, the Himalayas grow by about

6 centimetres
(2.4 inches) per year.

The eruption of Indonesia's Mount Tambora in 1815 was the largest ever recorded. The explosion was heard more than

1,930

kilometres (1,200 miles) away, and at least 71,000 people were killed.

When lava first spews from a volcano, it can be as hot as 700–1,200° Celsius (1,300–2,200 degrees Fahrenheit) It can flow across the land at speeds of up to

65 kilometres (40 miles) per hour!

Oceans

Oceans cover more than two-thirds of Earth's surface, but we have only explored a small part of their area. They are home to many different animals, and even plants. The waters of the oceans are constantly moving, and they help to keep Earth's climate stable.

The deeper into the oceans you go, the darker it gets. The pressure also increases, because of the enormous weight of the water above pressing down. Because of this, few animals can live in the deepest parts of the ocean.

The top layer of the ocean is called the sunlight zone, and it goes down to about 200 metres (660 miles). This is where most ocean life is found. Beneath it is the twilight zone. Here there is still some faint sunlight, but not enough for plants to grow. Below that is the midnight zone, then the abyssal zone, where it is always dark and few animals can survive.

EARTH BY NUMBERS

The ocean floor looks a bit like land on the surface, with deep canyons and tall mountains. Much of the ocean floor is covered with muddy **sediment**, made from the remains of plants and animals as well as ash and worn-down rocks.

The warm temperatures and light of the sunlight zone make a great habitat for corals, fish and other plants and animals.

In some places on the ocean floor, hydrothermal vents release hot water containing lots of minerals. The vents are home to some unusual creatures.

Lakes

A lake is an area of water that is surrounded by land. There are millions of lakes on Earth: some are small enough to fit in a back garden, while others are hundreds of kilometres across. The smallest lakes are often called ponds, and the largest are sometimes called seas. Some lakes are shallow enough to walk across, but Lake Baikal in Russia is more than 1.6 kilometres (1 mile) deep in places!

Many lakes were formed by glaciers that carved out hollows in the land as they moved along. When the glaciers melted, the water filled the hollows to create lakes. Other lakes were formed by the movement of tectonic plates, or when a river changed its course.

The water in most lakes is fresh water, but some contain salt water. Most saltwater lakes do not have rivers leading out of them. The only way for water to leave the lake is by **evaporation**, which usually leaves salt behind.

EARTH BY NUMBERS

Once a volcano is no longer active, sometimes its **crater** fills with rain or melted snow. Other volcanoes may have their top sections blown off in an eruption. This leaves a hollowed-out area called a caldera, which then fills with water.

Many of the lakes in North America were formed about 18,000 years ago, when glaciers last covered the land.

Lake Pinatubo in the Philippines formed in a caldera that was created by a huge eruption in 1991. It is now the country's deepest lake.

BODIES OF WATER—BY NUMBERS!

Lake Baikal's surface area of

31,600

square kilometres
(12,200 sq miles) is less than half
the size of Lake Superior. But it is four
times as deep and holds nearly as
much water as all five of
North America's Great Lakes
combined!

Out of all
the water on Earth, more than

96

per cent of it is found in the oceans.
They contain 1.3 billion cubic kilometres
(321 million cubic miles) of water!
Only 0.013 per cent of Earth's
water is found in lakes.

The world's biggest lake
by area is the Caspian Sea
in Asia, with an area of about

385,900

square kilometres (149,000 sq miles).
That's about the same size as Germany!

The tallest volcano on Earth is Ojos del Salado, on the border between Argentina and Chile. In its crater is a small lake, about **10** metres (33 feet) deep and 100 metres (328 feet) in diameter. It is probably the highest lake in the world.

The Mariana Trench is found in the Pacific Ocean. It is more than **2,540** kilometres (1,580 miles) long and 70 kilometres (43 miles) wide on average. Its deepest point is believed to be 10,990 metres (36,070 feet) below the surface.

The temperature at the surface of the oceans can be anywhere between -2 – 36° Celsius (28 – 97 degrees Fahrenheit). In the midnight zone, the temperature stays steady at about **4°** Celsius (39° Fahrenheit).

Rivers

When water moves across the land in a natural stream, it is called a river. A small river may be just a few kilometres long, while others flow for thousands of kilometres. Some only flow for part of the year, when heavy rain or melting snow fills them. Rivers flow downhill, from high ground to lower ground.

Rivers help to shape Earth's surface. They can carve out valleys and canyons as they flow over the land, wearing away rocks, soil and other sediment. They carry that sediment across the land, which creates fertile plains for growing crops. They also form part of the **water cycle**, taking water back to the oceans after it falls as rain.

Humans use rivers, too. We use their water for drinking and washing, and we use boats on rivers to transport people and goods for long distances. Rivers are also important habitats for many different plants and animals, from fish to dolphins.

The darker waters of the Rio Negro join the Amazon River as it flows across South America, before entering the Pacific Ocean.

Victoria Falls is located at one of the widest points of the Zambezi River. So much water goes over the falls that it is called "the smoke that thunders".

When a river's course takes it over a cliff, it can form a spectacular waterfall. Some waterfalls, such as Angel Falls in Venezuela, are incredibly tall. Others, such as Victoria Falls in Africa, are much shorter but very wide.

Canyons

Canyons can be some of Earth's most beautiful landforms. Many of these deep, narrow valleys are formed when a river travels over the land. The enormous weight of a river's water can cut deep into the riverbed. The water carries sediment from the riverbed downstream, making the channel wider.

The steep, rocky sides of canyons are usually caused by **weathering** and **erosion**. When rocks are worn away or broken down, this is called weathering. It can be caused by chemicals in rain that eat away at the rock, or by water getting into cracks in the rocks and then freezing and expanding. This breaks up the rock. When the pieces of rock are washed away, it is called erosion.

Canyons can also be formed by the collision of tectonic plates, making part of Earth's crust rise up higher than the land around it. Rivers flowing through this higher land can carve deep canyons.

EARTH BY NUMBERS

A slot canyon is a type of canyon that is much deeper than it is wide. Some of them are only a few metres across at the top! They were formed when fast-flowing water travelled through a narrow crack in the rock.

In this slot canyon, the water has carved the soft rock into beautiful flowing patterns.

The Colorado River cuts through an area of land in Arizona, USA, that was pushed up by tectonic plates. Over millions of years, the river carved out deep canyons.

RIVERS—BY NUMBERS!

Many sources say that the River Nile is

6,650

kilometres (4,132 miles) long, and the Amazon River is 6,399 kilometres (3,976 miles) long. It is hard to measure the length of a river, however, and some figures for the Amazon are as high as 6,840 kilometres (4,250 miles). No one can agree whether the Amazon or the Nile is the world's longest river.

Rivers are an important source of fresh water. More than

50 million

people live within a few kilometres of the River Nile, and they depend on its water.

Rivers can be measured by their discharge, which is the total amount of water flowing past a point. The average discharge of the Amazon River is

209,000

cubic metres (7,381,000 cubic feet) per second. The next six rivers on the list, added together, total only 205,095 cubic metres (7,243,000 cubic feet) per second!

The world's highest waterfall is Angel Falls in Venezuela, which drops a total of

979

metres (3, 212 feet).

The Grand Canyon in the United States is 445 kilometres (277 miles) long, 29 kilometres (18 miles) wide, and 1,830 metres (6,000 feet) deep. But it is not the world's longest or deepest canyon. The Yarlung Zangbo Grand Canyon in China is 499 kilometres (310 miles) long and in some places it is more than

5,331

metres (17,490 feet) deep.

Islands

An island is a body of land that is completely surrounded by water. **Continents** are also surrounded by water, but they are too big to be called islands. The world's largest island, Greenland, covers 2,165,000 square kilometres (836,000 sq miles), but the smallest continent, Australia, is about 7.8 million square kilometres (3 million sq miles).

Islands can be found all over the world, in oceans, lakes or rivers. They are often found in clusters called archipelagoes. Some islands are tiny with no people living there, and others are home to millions of people.

Some islands were once joined to a continent, but were separated when tectonic plates shifted. Others formed when sea levels rose, filling in lower land that joined them to the mainland. Barrier islands form along coastlines, when sand and other sediment pile up. They help protect the coast from storms. Some islands far out in the oceans are the tops of volcanoes rising from the ocean floor.

EARTH BY NUMBERS

People can create islands, too. They make them when they drain wet land, or bring in sand or other material from elsewhere.

Artificial islands have been created for hundreds of years. Many were built to make more space for people to live or grow crops.

The Palm Jumeirah in Dubai is an artificial island that was created to look like a palm tree.

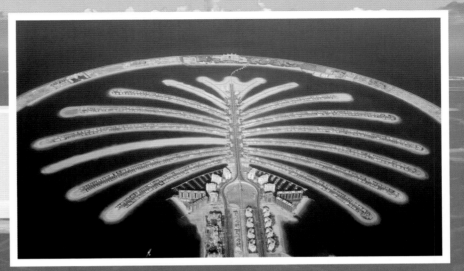

Some islands, such as this one in the Maldives, are formed by living creatures. Corals build up hard outer skeletons, which can break the surface of the water to form islands.

Caves

Some of Earth's most amazing landforms are beneath the surface. A cave is a natural opening in the ground that is large enough for a person to enter it. Some caves are small, single chambers, and others are long, narrow, twisting passages. Some caves have enormous underground chambers.

Caves can form in different types of rock. Many are found in a type of landscape called karst. This is a mixture of rocks including limestone, which can be dissolved by water containing a small amount of acid. Rainwater is slightly acidic, and when it seeps through the soil it becomes more acidic. Over thousands of years, it can wear away large areas of rock.

Some caves have amazing rock formations. Stalactites are like icicles made of rock that hang from the ceiling of a cave. Stalagmites grow up from the floor. Both of these features are formed from minerals in the water that slowly drips from the roof of the cave.

Some caves are enormous. The "Big Room" at Carlsbad Caverns in New Mexico, USA, is 550 metres (1,800 feet) long, with a ceiling 70 metres (225 feet) high.

Inside a cave it is usually dark and wet. Many of the animals that live in caves have special **adaptations** for living there. Some are blind, but they have developed other senses that help them. For example, one type of cavefish can find food by feeling vibrations in the water.

Stalagmites often form from water that drips down a stalactite and falls to the floor.

A home for all

Our planet is more than just a collection of landforms. Earth is also home to a lot of different landscapes, from deserts and polar ice caps to rainforests and prairies. Each landscape is part of a different **ecosystem**, where many different plants and animals live.

Animals and plants live together in ecosystems. An ecosystem can be small, such as a pond, or large, such as a forest. The animals and plants that live there depend on each other. For example, plants in a meadow ecosystem may provide food and homes for caterpillars, beetles and grasshoppers. These insects are eaten by birds, which may be eaten by larger birds or other animals.

All ecosystems are different, and plants and animals have adaptations to survive the conditions where they live. For example, some fish that live in the deepest, darkest parts of the ocean are able to make light with their bodies. This helps them attract prey.

EARTH BY NUMBERS

Animals and plants in deserts have adaptations that help them to survive in a hot, dry climate. Kangaroo rats dig burrows where they can stay cool, and they don't need to drink at all – they can get all the moisture they need from the seeds they eat!

A grassland such as this one in Africa can be home to many different species of plants and animals.

Rainforests are one of the richest habitats on Earth, so it is important to protect them.

Glossary

adaptations changes in an organism, over time, that help it survive and reproduce in a particular habitat

canyons narrow valleys with steep sides, often with a stream or river flowing through them

cliffs very steep vertical faces of rock or ice

continents Earth's seven major landmasses

crater bowl-shaped hollow around the opening of a volcano

crust the hard, rocky outer layer of Earth

deserts very dry, sandy or rocky areas with very few plants growing in them

dormant not currently active. Many volcanoes can lie dormant for hundreds of years before erupting.

ecosystem community of living things, together with their environment

erosion process by which loosened material is worn away from rocks

erupt send out rocks, ash, lava and gas in a sudden explosion

evaporation turning from a liquid into a gas

fertile able to support the growth of plants

fjords narrow inlets of the sea, found between cliffs or steep slopes

glaciers large masses of ice that move very slowly down a slope or across land

habitats natural environments of animals or plants

lava molten rock that comes out of a volcano

magma molten rock beneath Earth's surface

molten turned into liquid because of high temperatures

prairies large, flat areas of land covered mainly in grasses

rainforests dense woodlands with very high rainfall each year, often with trees forming a canopy

sediment tiny pieces of rock, soil and other materials that are carried by flowing water

tectonic plates large sections of Earth's crust. Tectonic plates are constantly colliding with or moving away from other plates.

volcanoes mountains with a hole in the top or sides that can send out rocks, ash, lava and gas in an eruption

water cycle cycle in which Earth's water turns from vapour in the air into rain or other precipitation and falls to the ground, where it is collected and evaporates again

weathering wearing away of rock by chemical, physical or biological processes

Find out more

Books

Earth: The Definitive Visual Guide, DK (DK, 2013)

Exploring Rivers: A Benjamin Blog and His Inquisitive Dog Investigation (Exploring Habitats with Benjamin Blog and His Inquisitive Dog), Anita Ganeri (Raintree, 2015)

Mountains (Explorer Travel Guides), Chris Oxlade (Raintree, 2014)

Rainforests (Explorer Travel Guides), Nick Hunter (Raintree, 2014)

Volcanoes (DKfindout!), DK (DK Children, 2016)

Websites

Watch this video about rivers and the water cycle:
www.bbc.co.uk/education/clips/zb39jxs

Find out more about caves at:
www.dkfindout.com/uk/earth/caves/

Find out more about different types of glaciers, and how glaciers change the land, at:
www.dkfindout.com/uk/earth/glaciers/

Index

Andes Mountains 10
Angel Falls 19, 23
animals 4, 12, 18, 27, 28
Australia 24

canyons 4, 12, 18, 20–21, 23
Caspian Sea 16
caves 4, 26–27
cliffs 4, 19
climate 12, 28

deserts 4, 28

ecosystems 28
erosion 20
evaporation 14

fish 18, 27, 28

glaciers 7, 14
Grand Canyon 4, 23
Greenland 24

Hawaii 8
hotspots 8

islands 8, 24–25

Lake Baikal 14, 16
lakes 4, 14–15, 16, 17, 24
Lake Superior 16
lava 8, 11

Mariana Trench 17
mid-ocean ridge 10
Moon 4
mountains 4, 6–7, 8, 10–11, 12
Mount Everest 6
Mount Tambora 11

ocean floor 12, 24
oceans 4, 8, 10, 12–13, 16, 17, 18, 24, 28
Ojos de Salado 17

plains 4, 18
planets 4
plants 4, 12, 18, 28
prairies 4, 28

rain 14, 18, 20, 26
rainforests 4, 28
River Nile 22
rivers 4, 7, 14, 18–19, 20, 22, 23, 24

snow 6, 14, 18
stalactites and stalagmites 26

tectonic plates 6, 8, 10, 11, 14, 20, 24

valleys 4, 6–7, 18, 20
volcanoes 4, 8–9, 11, 14, 17, 24

water cycle 18
waterfalls 19, 23
weathering 20

Yarlung Zangbo Grand Canyon 23